Treasures from the Heart

Treasures from the Heart

Poems

Elizabeth Zara Pagan

iUniverse, Inc.
New York Lincoln Shanghai

Treasures from the Heart

iUniverse books may be ordered through booksellers or by contacting:

iUniverse
2021 Pine Lake Road, Suite 100
Lincoln, NE 68512
www.iuniverse.com
1-800-Authors (1-800-288-4677)

ISBN-13: 978-0-595-39608-5 (pbk)
ISBN-13: 978-0-595-84311-4 (cloth)
ISBN-13: 978-0-595-84011-3 (ebk)
ISBN-10: 0-595-39608-9 (pbk)
ISBN-10: 0-595-84311-5 (cloth)
ISBN-10: 0-595-84011-6 (ebk)

Printed in the United States of America

I dedicate this book to my wonderful husband, Rey, without whose support this book would not have become a reality.

Contents

PART III NATURE AND ITS WONDER

Acknowledgments

I would like to thank my wonderful husband, Rey Pagan, for giving me the stamina to write not only from nine to five, but from dawn to dusk. Without his support, this book could not have been possible.

I thank the joy and pride of my life, my sons, Joe and Rey Jr., for believing in me.

I also thank my uncle, Francisco Reyes, for truly believing I could write from my heart.

To all my readers, enjoy. I give you my many thanks.

Elizabeth Zara Pagan

Introduction

While vacationing in Washington DC, I visited many historical sites, one of which was the Tomb of the Unknown located in Arlington National Cemetery, Arlington, Virginia. The site was very peaceful and quiet out of respect to the Unknown Soldier buried there.

I sat as close as possible near the guard in arms with the hope of not missing the changing of the guards. As the soldier stood guarding the tomb, I noticed the white rectangular tomb with columns set into the surface. While I could not see the markings in the back of the tomb, I knew it read:

HERE RESTS
IN HONORED GLORY
AN AMERICAN SOLDIER
KNOWN BUT TO GOD.

Tears ran down my cheeks as I thought of how this soldier, unknown as he may be, had given his life to protect our own. I became emotional. I was so strongly inspired to write again that as soon as I returned home from my vacation, I immediately sat down in front of my personal computer and generated a poem called "Soldier Unknown." As my husband read this poem, I could see he was deeply touched.

"Soldier Unknown" is a poem about a young woman who visits the Arlington National Cemetery and stumbles upon a soldier's grave. She wonders why this brave soldier gave his life and imagines how his loved ones must have felt losing their brave soldier to battle. She then hears a voice that apparently reads her thoughts and gives his answer as to why he gave his own life. The writing of this poem further inspired me to write.

"Soldier Unknown" earned recognition and was published by the International Library of Poetry; it was also given the Editor's Choice Award for Outstanding Achievement in Poetry.

Writing comes to me naturally because I write with my emotions. I take pleasure in reading the writings of my favorite poet, Edgar Allan Poe. I look forward to writing further since it is my passion to write.

I currently live in Poughkeepsie, New York, and was raised in the lower east side of Manhattan. I am a married mother of two sons and have two adorable grandchildren.

I truly hope you enjoy reading my book as much as I enjoyed writing it.

Elizabeth Zara Pagan

ELIZABETH

Edgar Allan Poe
(1850)

Elizabeth, it surely is most fit
[Logic and common usage so commanding]
In thy own book that first thy name be writ,
Zeno and other sages notwithstanding;
And I have other reasons for so doing
Besides my innate love of contradiction;
Each poet—if a poet—in pursuing
The muses thro' their bowers of Truth or Fiction,
Has studied very little of his part,
Read nothing, written less—in short's a fool
Endued with neither soul, nor sense, nor art,
Being ignorant of one important rule,
Employed in even the theses of the school—
Called—I forget the heathenish Greek name
[Called anything, its meaning is the same]
"Always write first things uppermost in the heart."

I

Patriotic

The Battle for Freedom

From the mountain near the sea, I guarded our territorial reserve as I scoped the enemy below. I tried to rest my eyes but then heard a tremendous roar coming from the distance. Men, women, and children ran back and forth, trying their best to distance themselves from the dangers that surrounded them as they scampered to take shelter, running away from what haunted them.

We readied ourselves to do battle against our enemy as we looked around and consumed all that surrounded us. Cautiously we made it to the fields, the roar of thunder getting nearer. We readied ourselves to maim and conquer. We aimed our weapons toward the enemy and fought with vigor as mortar combat kept increasing.

While our aircraft carried out their bombing run, we heard more explosions here and there, lighting the night as day, and on we fought until dawn. We saw our enemy lying wounded or dead.

With danger in every corner lurking, we continued onward, ever knowing that fighting was not optional. It was essential, for freedom was not free.

Soldier Unknown

I walk this misty, moonless night,
This darkened night with starless skies.
No silhouette cast by my side,
In the quiet of this peaceful sight.

Crosses were similar in width and height,
Appeared simple, the crosses were white
Carefully arranged in perfect formation,
A monumental statue stood in commemoration.

I noticed a tombstone thus recluse,
This tombstone near the Norway spruce,
Bearing the words, "Here rests a soldier unknown.
He died with honor, but not alone."

I thought of those he had left behind,
His children, his wife, his love divine.
I bowed my head, heaved a sigh and cried
For this soldier who had bravely died.

Then I heard a voice that said,
"The fight I fought, I did not dread.
The life I gave was not in vain;
For your freedom, I would die again."

And as I looked toward the Norway tree,
I thanked this soldier for keeping me free,
The life he gave to free my own
From this soldier who remains unknown.

Taps

Loud haunting echo of Taps was heard
In the coldness of twilight nigh,
While the silent dead were put to sleep
By the haunting song of Taps.

Safely resting the heroes nigh,
We mourned our fallen braves.
The silent son, the many slept,
Thy mother's grief, the many wept.

As Taps beckoned us to remember
Their lives lost to hold us free,
In gratitude to them we were,
Would always in memory be.

While death walked on no-man's-land,
The many slept, the many wept.
The bugle call of Taps was heard
While we slept, a mother's son nigh…
The haunting song of Taps.

From Day to Darkness

How sad the nation when the World's Twin,
In the month of September the 11th day wherein,
Aircrafts used as weapons of mass destruction,
Annihilate both Towers by its aggression.

Active pedestrians everywhere is to say,
Walk under no cloud of gloom foretells a pleasant day,
When a thunderous blast were heard from the sky,
Streets filled with people gather with somber eyes.

Spectators gaze with attention and yet,
Not knowing the peril, it beset,
From the sky, a jet plane hit the first Tower,
People are stunned as they watch in horror.

Then more explosions on a massive scale,
The second plane struck Tower 2 without fail,
Vast shattered stones are dropping from the rise,
As the watcher's cry of Armageddon are seen in their eyes,

Sirens is heard from every direction,
As rescuers, urgently struggle to hasten,
To assist dwellers of Towers 1 and 2,
Immediately get there to search and rescue.

Frantic cries is heard as it arched across the sky,
As creeping flames of scarlet, intensify,
Redeemers heroically attempt to salvage,
Every one trapped from Towers bondage.

Then the roar, rattle, groan and grinding,
Twisting metal, windows blowing, Tower 2 is collapsing,
With their last breath taken people are jumping,
Tower 2 is descending like a speeding train rumbling.

Tower1 rapidly follow then smoke of cloud,
It rain debris covered by the sky's gray shroud,
Blinding the air with ashes pitch black,
As all is no more from the terrorist attack.

While all around silence and falling debris,
Survivors wander in gloom some fall to their knees,
Weeping and confounded while others assist,
Gone Towers 1 and 2 no longer exist.

Whereas the world watches hence strikingly shaken,
Of countless lives lost by enemy taken,
The heavenly light befall whole and white,
While angels host their souls to the beam of light.

The Terror Within

While I faced the traffic light
On this overcrowded street,
My body temperature rises
To the scorching summer heat.

I sense I am late, cannot hesitate,
This meeting is so vital.
With signal green, I start to cross,
And proceeded to my recital.

As I am walking, I hear a blast,
An explosion of some sort.
People scampering to take shelter,
Running toward the food court.

I joined the many people scuttling.
While I scampered, I turned to see,
A burning bus, people strewn,
About the ground among debris.

I noticed I was surrounded
By the wounded and the dead.
I imagined it a war zone,
I feared what was ahead.

I heard the sirens from afar,
To aid the wounded, those that are.
While some lie still, motionless,
Those souls that were corpus,

I heard a woman's cry for help,
Felt her fear from within.
I saw blood on her everywhere,
Her face, her body, her skin.

As I hasten to her side
To aid her though in fear,
I held her closely to comfort her,
To tell her help was near.

With trepidation visible,
The dreadful terror in her eyes,
I tried with all my might to hide,
My terror within, this terror inside.

As she took her last breath, I shed my tears,
For her soul, the wounded, those dead,
I prayed God to cradle her in His arms,
As I cried more tears of dread.

93
Not Just a Number

In the morning of nine eleven,
The passengers of Flight 93,
Had no idea what would happen to them,
When their lives ended tragically

On a nice September morning,
Not a cloud of puffy white could they see,
It was warm like early summer teasing,
When passengers and crew took off on United 93

Shortly after their departure, clearly,
They heard a commotion up ahead,
Passengers wondered what it could be,
"We have a problem," someone said.

They turned their heads in that direction,
Saw a man standing near the way,
Another threatened without hesitation,
To kill them if they did not obey,

Passengers in awe saw a man bludgeon,
Seriously wounded about the head,
Their hearts pounded, became frightened,
As the man's head continued to bleed.

They heard a woman's repeated screams,
As her voice echoed throughout the plane,
It seemed like a nightmare, a bad dream,
When her cries became silent, ending her pain.

Anxiously, passengers called their loved ones,
While others looked around in dread,
"I love you," "Good-bye," "Held hostage," they said,
They imagined themselves dead.

With danger in every corner lurking,
Passengers conveyed their information,
"The Twin Towers and Pentagon…gone,"
They whispered in desperation.

Passengers and crew discussed their plan,
"We must take them just the same,
Let's attack now, before it's too late,"
They planned to hurt and to maim.

Then a man yelled out, "Let's roll!"
As the others set themselves ready to combat,
United they stood, with weapons of this and that,
Against their rival, they attacked.

They ran and screamed, plowed ahead,
Like a banshee, louder, loudening,
They crashed into the terrorists,
Wounding their opponent, fighting,

They rammed the food cart into the cockpit door,
Shouting to do harm and confound,
They collided, crashed, smashed some more,
Faster, closer, nearer, downed…
Silence…

To Conquer, Divine

There are those who are unstable,
Evil, hateful, carnage able,
Desire to eradicate our nation,
From their abhorrence without hesitation.

These extremists self-proclaimed
Maintain to invade and to maim,
Capitulate, execute, and impair,
Aim to hurt us and to scare.

Our braves have died not in vain,
Loved ones have lost, suffered pain,
Pledged their lives to never surrender,
Knowing freedom has its danger.

We stand united without divide,
Will waver not, for conquer is divine,
For liberty, justice, and 9/11,
We battle for freedom and the vault of heaven.

Candle of Hope

Held in bondage thus confined,
A room hence tiny holds my fate,
I live in fear of darkness, lost,
Cannot let the candlelight exhaust.

I pray and pray, no rescue comes,
My life but short, I want to live.
Save me from this shadowed death,
Before the candle of hope's last breath.

II

Pleasure and Pain

Treasures from the Heart

Treasures from the heart are many,
From gold to priceless art;
Adversity or triumph of everyday life,
We feel emotion of the heart.

Love is like a rose in time,
Blooms to beauty as it grows,
Becomes a timeless treasure,
Like a delicate old garden rose.

The memories you share
Amid your family and friends,
They are valuable tools of love,
That will hold you until the end.

But if you're sad and lonely,
If you are given a loving embrace,
Hold your timeless treasure,
Hence, your heart will mend.

Because I Care

The loneliness bestowed upon me,
Is dreadfully felt without thee,
To think of you, to see you smile,
You are all that make life worthwhile.

But if one day you should need me,
Because I care I will be near,
No need to either pain or fear,
Nor shed your precious tear.

I Think of Thee

In total darkness I think of thee,
By candlelight to guide me see,
My broken heart for thee still stings,
Gone you are no longer with me.

I drink a glass of Cabernet
To greet my love in his azure eyes,
I see my memory's hazy smoke
Disappear in the sky of hope.

As darkness thickens, blinding me,
My tears streaming wet for thee,
You are gone, never will I see,
In darkness, I grieve for thee.

A New Beginning

Never can I fill your heart with yearning,
Am I not all you want me to be?
Forever in mine eyes the lamp is burning,
My eyes of gloom still pain for thee.

Tell not this dishearten heart,
Your love for me but fades away,
My ruptured heart thus torn apart,
Yet hope again my life portray.

If such time you love again,
The mask you wear of grin and lies,
Will turn love to hate from any woman,
From your cruel intent to pain then cries.

Weep not my heart of yesterday,
My past sorrow shall not win,
I will start my new day,
Of my life, anew begin.

Romancing the Night

Soft candlelight gently burning,
Will guide our love this night,
Emit shadows gently turning,
Help romance this night alight.

Our shadows join us as we dance,
Romantically by candlelight,
His luscious lips soft on mine,
Kissed me tenderly, held me tight.

Dotingly we dance to the romantic song,
Our hearts beat as one, whereon,
Romance this special night ignites,
We dance from dusk to dawn.

Crimson Rose

I'm not content to live divided,
I shed my cries of useless tears,
Dark clouds, I am brokenhearted,
I cannot abandon my heart to fear.

Mere shadow of my love you are,
My heart of brightness best,
You are so far away, like the star,
My love for you transcends.

Loving smiles of sweet surrender,
Soft, delicate to the touch are those,
The beauty of our love the splendor,
Is like the beautiful crimson rose.

Remember Me

Remember me when I depart,
I will not forget you.

Remember me when you are brokenhearted,
I will mend your heart.

Remember me when you are lonely,
I will be by your side.

Remember me when you're in pain, my only,
I will always comfort you.

Remember me when you miss my embrace,
I will always hold you.

Remember me when you miss my love,
I will always love you.

Remember me and our life together,
For our life will always be.

Remember me when your time is near,
I will wait for you.

From the Heavens (I Hear Your Cries)

I hear your cry of agony,
Many sufferings bestowed upon thee,
The numerous pains you have endured,
From the heavens, I hear your cries.

Do not despair my child,
Do not fear for I am with thee,
For my door shall be open,
I hear your cries in me.

Thou not be lost my child,
I shall guide thee for I am the light,
I will welcome you in my house,
You will ache and cry no more…

The Vision

Little Jessica seven in her room, played,
Saw a vision when to her it called,
From the wall the light originated,
Emerged as Jessica became enthralled,

The translucent woman walked with care,
Wore a long veil of richest blue,
It covered her silky dark long hair,
Her face hence white, it was pure.

She looked toward Jessica caringly,
With eyes as dark as night,
Her face glowing like the Beauty,
Surrounded her with emanating light,

Lovingly the woman spoke to her,
"I come to warn of danger ahead,
In the wall a fire shall be, aver,
As you sleep this night," she said.

While seeing the vision by the wall,
Jessica wonders who this could be,
"Who are you that come to call?"
"My child", she said, "I am called Mary".

That night of dreadful dark,
Smoke spread about as Jessica slept,
Then the fire followed by a spark,
"Wake my child, said Mary to awake.

From slumber Jessica suddenly awaken,
To what was lurking in the night,
Cried for help, and was shaken,
When saved from her dangerous plight.

While Jessica safely stood by her loved ones,
She turned her head as she looked on,
Saw the Lady as she said with pleasance,
"You are blessed my child," then she was gone.

My Bells Toll for Thee

If ever two bodies became one,
Such love as ever sweet and tender,
The bells that toll for each of us,
Announce our love forever,
My bells toll for thee.

You fill my heart and quench my thirst,
Your given breath, the breath of love,
Makes me want to soar the sky,
Like a beautiful white dove.
My bells still toll for thee.

Celebrate Your Love to Me

Do you celebrate your love to me?
In body, soul, and heart,
Instill your want, and still decree
We will never be apart.

For time passes us rapidly by,
We have so much to give,
Respect, love, and honor,
The readiness to forgive.

Will I celebrate myself to you?
My heart may tell me so.
I am not sure if I would renew
Our vows, I do not know.

But if you celebrate your love to me,
And have been always true,
Then for our diamond jubilee,
I will remarry you.

Will I celebrate my life with you?
Yes, delightedly each day,
I pray God will bless us both,
Guide us all the way.

The Lovebirds

While tanning under the searing sun,
I saw a couple stroll by lovingly,
Contentedly walking hand in hand
I watched them inquisitively.

They climbed atop a boulder
They sat under the cloudless sky.
He passionately kissed her lips,
While the birds zipped by from up high,

Then up they went together,
Walking amorously hand in hand,
I looked on curiously, spying,
As the lovebirds walked the scorching sand.

Best to Part

See in mine eyes the look of love,
Disdain to waste one look on me,
Your heart of stone, I will not seek,
You fade away so to speak.

My life yet bent upside down,
I lost the heart I thought I found,
Do no my soul betray, by your own,
Best to part and I left alone.

Hence if I but love again,
My heart but thinks twice and when,
For every woman there is a man,
For every man thinks he can.

Vows

Amorously you proposed to me,
Held my hand, knelt on your knee,
Met mine eyes and with pride
Invited me to be your bride,

With fingers crossed, you heard me say,
"I'll marry you this very day."
Jubilant you were, so amazed,
Adoringly gave me your embrace.

"Love, honor, and cherish without falter,
In sickness and in health," was said at the altar.
With promises made, we gave the Lord our word,
We said, "I do," and our Lord heard.

Life

From within the heart is one,
Your breath of life, I give to thee,
Take thy heart and treasure life,
Live your life in harmony.

To the Heavens

We counted the stars, you and I,
We shared our love with pleasure and pride,
You will always be my shining knight,
Forever will be my guiding light.

If only you were here with me,
You are gone, and never can you be,
Thus, I am lost without thee,
Of wanting thee to not say good-bye.

The stars I see sparkling above,
I close mine eyes and think of thee,
Thus, send you my undying love,
To the heavens, I send my heart to thee.

A Whisper in the Wind

I hear a whisper in the wind,
Bellowing through the dampened grass,
Lurking in the shadows of night,
I close mine eyes of pains and tears,
From the night's past and hidden fears,
Buried deep within my mind,
Of past treasures left behind.
In the bottomless shadows of the night,
The children sleep their lullaby,
Cradled by the whispering wind,
Then quietly the wind snuggle down,
Fares good night and goes to sleep,
Gone is the whisper in the wind.

You Are All I Need

Love, like the mighty tide ebbs and flows,
Through my soul like a river to the sea,
When I hear your soft voice,
My heart leaps at the whisper of your name.
Your sweet lips of lush berries quench my thirst.
I wait in the moonlight in search of the splendid cobalt sky,
That we may exist as one and never part,
My heart you are all I need.

Until We Meet Again

Whilst the train announces to depart,
Mine eyes but crave to see,
My husband, my loving heart,
I wish him here with me.

I never lost as much but twice,
His love and his precious life,
Then I clutch my duffel bag,
And proceed to board the train.

Glancing out the window, I see,
Him standing over there,
His face so sad and lonely,
It is more than I can bear.

Then I realize he is gone,
As tears stream down my face,
Gradually he fades away, beyond,
He has gone to a higher place.

While I gaze upon the beauty,
Of the trees and countryside,
My heart suffers silent pain,
Until we meet again.

My Loving Heart

My loving heart, I say with pride,
The love I have for you inside
Is greater than you'll ever know,
It is just as strong as years ago.

In your arms you shelter me,
You comfort me I shed no tears,
Like a book of holy prayer,
You take away all my fears.

When I am lonely all day long,
Because I miss you when you are gone,
I count the hours and minutes too,
Just to spend another day with you.

Hence you, my love, I still adore,
Every day I love you more,
You are the world to me, my life,
I am proud to be your wife.

With Appreciation

My dear husband, to you I convey
My concerns for you in every way,
Burdens you have carried, your sacrifices made,
As you face the challenges before you each day.

Hard worker, supportive you remain,
A father, a husband, and still maintain
To dedicate yourself to us unselfishly,
You give yourself totally, devotedly, absolutely.

It pains me to see you look fatigued,
A tough day's work, one more day achieved,
Getting no rest, lacking the sleep you need,
It makes it difficult for you to succeed.

Each morning you rise to work your day,
Commuting for hours and to my dismay,
Whether it be snowing, sleeting, or raining,
Forward you go without complaining.

Admired you are, you are treasured,
Adored, appreciated, and respected.
I love you more each day,
With appreciation my love I sincerely convey.

You Light Up My Life

Grandchildren are special in every way,
When they smile, like the sun it warms my heart,
When their eyes shine with laughter,
The stars luminosity light up my life,
When they give me their hug,
I melt like the snow in the spring.
To all treasured memories, sweet memories,
I hold them dearly in my heart.

Little Children Lost

Little children lost in the fearsome forest and wind,
Felt lonely, lost and frightened,
In the silence of the shadowed night,
The children began to sob with fright.

They rested their eyes on a shining brilliance,
A glowing light, pure and white,
Watched as it approached them with its kindness,
To protect and lead them home this nigh.

Hear the Children Cry

Hear the children cry,
From within the dark nearby,
Their souls roam the earth with fright,
In the shadow of the night,

Hear the children cry,
Their precious life gone by,
Evil's weed casting blow,
For reasons we will never know,

Their souls we lay to unending sleep,
With grief and pain we deeply weep,
We pray to the Lord the children blessed,
To cradle in His arms to rest.

Children Play

I noticed a child as I was walking,
With her friend, she was chatting,
Someone just about her age,
She had a smile on her little face.

She was maybe three foot two,
Eyes bright, like the ocean, blue,
With somewhat silky, long blond hair,
Her skin looked creamy and fair.

Her friend's height was much like hers,
Eyes were brown and not like the other girl's,
Her hair was auburn with long curls
With skin darker than the other girl's.

While the children played, having fun
Under the brightness of the sun,
They sang a song and clapped their hands,
They danced in concert on the sand.

Then someone called them by their names,
It was time to go, no more playing games,
The girls turned and smiled as I looked on,
Said "Good-bye," and then they were gone.

Angels Rise

While angels rise to a crescendo, loudening
Chorus of voices in concert, singing,
Chanting their praise to the above,
Serenading our Lord with all their love.

When our time draws near and we must go,
Heavenly angels, their trumpets they will blow,
Announcing our arrival to heaven's gate,
As they open the door to our Lord's estate.

Sons of Mine

It is amazing how I can think back
To the time when you were born,
When I would count your fingers and toes,
I hoped all ten were there.

When you took your first steps,
Wobbling from side to side
As you walked across the room,
I prayed you made it there.

Or when for the first time
You went to school, how proud I was,
When you carried your first backpack,
I felt lonely and in disrepair.

Now all grown up and married
With children of your own,
You count their fingers and their toes,
And hope all ten are there,
...Oh darling sons of mine.

How Great the Grief

How great the grief when all seems lost,
Of precious life forever tossed,
When spoken words are lies and grins,
Just thorns from needles and pins,

He will speak not a solemn word,
My silenced ears of words unheard,
If only an open wound can heal,
Then grief and pain I would not feel.

My Weeping Heart

My wilted rose, my weeping heart,
Wrong me not by your craving lust,
I will close mine heart, hence seal your lips,
I will not yield your tongue to trust.

Thus, if such lover as thee wrong me,
I will utter not a word of this or that,
To you of what is contained in memory,
I will not gaze at thee nor chat.

The Last Remaining Human

I gaze the inert sky of doom,
Nor life I see but death and tomb,
Not a bird soar the garnet skies,
All but gone before mine eyes,

While dazed I walk the streets and strive,
In search of food to survive,
Whilst deep within I grieve alone
My life is all I call my own.

I roam the earth lost in darkness,
Lonely, frightened and lifeless,
I live as the last remaining human,
There is no one to speak neither man nor woman.

Melody of Love

I heard a melody from afar,
The gentle strings of a guitar,
A heavenly sound, thus angelic,
Touched my heart with its magic.

The song grew softer as it played,
Stronger, louder, it became,
This romantic song played in the air,
Spreading its love everywhere.

When played with all its passion,
Charming melody filled with emotion
Made me passionately desire
All the love I could acquire.

While the evening slowly surrendered
To the darkness and its splendor,
Melody of love continued to play,
Scattering its affection along the way.

In Death I Mourn

Deeply weeping on your knees,
You cry in sympathy for me;
You plant a rose of deepest red,
To grow on my garden's bed.

You mourn for me, your passion seen,
Your silent words, no sound I hear;
Under the moon, the mountain sleeps,
As you shed your bitter tears.

My love thus kept in your heart
Will keep me with you, not apart,
Our Lord one day will call your name,
You will come to me, my loving heart.

Painful Reality

I walk the shores alone this night,
This dismal dark, I gaze at the sky,
I feel depressed and wonder why,
Tears of pain stream down my eyes.

In dread, I try to ascertain,
The reason why I am in pain,
As a child I was not as blessed,
Not like the others, not like the rest.

Life is brief, I see this now,
Do not know the years God will allow,
My stay on earth, with all His grace,
When He takes me to a higher place.

I know now that I must forgive,
Must forget so I can live,
I see there are others just like me,
Who have suffered pain and cannot be free.

The Secret

My secret kept I can now tell,
A secret I know too well,
Something I did not want you to know,
For it will surely hurt you so.

Scores of years hence passed away,
I carry shame 'til this day,
Was deeply hurt and frightened so,
Tell I will, so you will know.

How this happened you must know,
I cannot recall exactly, though,
The night was cold, it was not clear,
I walked home alone in fear.

A man toddled by that darkened night,
In the shadows he lurked in unlit light,
He casually walked next to me,
Without inviting him, you see.

I tried to run with all my might,
In that unlit and forsaken night,
He seized me, and could not contain
The fear I cannot explain.

I yelled and screeched but no one came,
My God, please help me attain
My strength to fight this man off me,
I cried, "Stop, please hear my plea."

He forced himself on me, on top,
I struggled fiercely, he would not stop,
He listened not, didn't hear my cry,
He felt my body, then my thigh.

I wept and begged him to let me be,
I pleaded God to set me free,
Then after he was set and done,
He ran and ran, then he was gone.

This secret I could not explain
To you, my love, of all my pain,
Then I thought why say a word
Of this horror that had occurred.

I have kept this secret deep inside,
For I was soon to be your bride,
I hope and pray you understand,
This was not something I had planned.

I have lived my life with all this shame,
This burden carried, I am not to blame,
I have suffered and I have cried,
Thus, I have wished I would have died.

I love you so, my tender dear,
I say this with all my heart and tear,
This took place, I will not deny,
It happened, I know not why.

Silent Tears

Deafening silence, you remain,
Signs of darkness, you maintain,
Your stillness held with no response,
Your demeanor was nonchalant.

Forever weep my silent tears
From within my thunderous fears,
With aloofness, hushed somewhat,
Yet wondering what if what was…was not.

My Heaven Sent

I walk this soundless night,
A quiet night with stars so bright,
Casting shadows everywhere,
Soft wind blowing in my hair.

I see a brilliance of white ahead,
I hear a pleasant voice that says,
"I am an angel, don't despair,
I'm here to guide you, not scare."

"You are my angel," I implore,
"I've never seen one quite before,
Please do not go, do not part,
Are you here to heal my heart?

"My heaven sent end my pain,
I hurt, I cry, and hurt again,
I am not valiant, I am not strong,
Can you please take me along?"

"Life is precious, don't you know,
Our Lord loves you ever so,
Have faith, be strong, I do implore,
The pain in you will be no more."

Fear

The wobbly dark of murky night,
I neither see nor hear,
I sense I am alone, but not quite,
As I walk down the hill with fear.

I try to see ahead of me
In the darkness, here and there,
I see a stone of someone's loss
That reads "Pass me if you dare."

The tremulous sound of eerie cries
Is heard above the large oak tree,
Then I see eminent glowing eyes,
While the owl stood over me.

With fear I pass the owl of night
As I stare behind me still,
In the dark beneath the twilight
The owl gives his deafening shrill.

I run with fright up the hill,
Away from this fear of night,
The hill, the silenced shrill,
I smiled and feared no more.

You Are Not Here

I know not what to do
When I awaken every morning,
You are not here.

I know not what to do
When my heart is empty, sad, and lonely,
You are not here.

I know not what to do
When I am cold and need your warmth,
You are not here.

I know not what to do
When the darkened night ends in fear,
You are not here.

I know not what do
When my bed is empty and I need your kiss,
You are not here.

I know not what to do
When I am lonely without you,
My love, now you are gone.

Forever Kept

How brave a woman to have raised alone,
Five children by her own,
With the power of love, her heart,
She kept them close, never apart.

When they cried, then sobs then fears,
Silently she shed her secret tears,
Like the beauty's guiding light,
Prayed profoundly for them every night,

Quietly she watched them sleep and then,
From within she prayed again,
To keep them safe away from harm,
From evil's weed casting blow.

Bless the silent hours, mourning,
Her children are somber weeping,
As they rest their mother's soul to sleep,
They pray the Lord her soul to keep,
In His arms forever kept.

Chipmunk Alvin

Nuisance Alvin cute and naughty,
Goes here and there fast and doughty,
In my garden everywhere,
He weaves around without a care.

With all my might I chase him down,
Then nuisance Alvin swirls around,
Quicker than a speeding train,
Into the hole, he goes again.

Annoyed I wait for him to show,
Then stares at me wiggle his nose,
Uncovers a gap here and there,
To beneath the earth I know not where.

Sleep Tonight

My child you lack your beauty sleep,
You fear the darkness as you keep,
Worry not for no one's there,
There is no need to fear or despair.

If you cannot sleep count to ten,
Close your eyes and then and when,
Your mind sees things that are not there,
Just think it is your mind playing fair.

Tell yourself not once but twice,
It will not hurt you nor entice,
Nothing to scare is there this night,
Just turn the switch and put on the light.

If still you scare just say your prayer,
You are safe, no need to fear,
No need to lose your beauty sleep,
You will soon be sound asleep.

The Coaster Ride

Excitedly, I sank into my seat
I readied for the ride and planted my feet
Leisurely the coaster ascended to the top
Approaching its near-vertical drop.

With lungs full of air, I closed my eyes
Proceeded to take the gut-wrenching ride
I screamed, I bellowed, held on with intensity
As it sped downward with increasing velocity.

Bumps, turns, here and there
The coaster continued riding on air
Then suddenly the car came to a screeching halt
I had left my stomach behind to a fault.

III

Nature and Its Wonder

The Wonders of Nature

While I inhale the sweet fragrance of a flower,
The air sweet after a morning shower,
Wind blows tenderly across the sea,
As it caresses my hair with a gentle tease.

The sky provides its heavenly rainbow,
From side to side with multicolored glow
Birds serenade the infinite indigo sky
In daylight as they flutter up high.

Clouds appear fluffy, color white,
Making the heavens a welcome sight
While the sun gives us its joy of brightness,
It glows radiantly with politeness.

The sun yet bright with blinding light
Reflects from the ocean with delight
While the azure water in its deep
Is clear, tranquil, and still asleep.

While I walk the scorching sand,
The sun still beating upon the land,
I feel the sensation of a tender breeze,
As it caresses my hair with a gentle tease.

Nature's Anger

While the skies turn ominous nigh,
Thunder roaring like the lion,
Light the sky on fire, red,
Heavy pours of water fallen.

I hear the fear by mine ears
While the sky threatens, scares,
Crash of anger everywhere,
Stars have gone, I know not where.

Against the rocks in anger, crashes,
Leaves, comes, and smacks the rock,
Again, again in anger smashes.
Lighting day when it's night by the dock.

Forever Lost

In the near waking storm,
A passing ship in darkness, seen,
In the shadows of hungry waters,
The blinding ocean of the deep,
The sinking ship sends up flairs of white,
Lighting the heavens with temporary light
In the shadow with no warning,
Their cries are heard, soul's unrest,
Pleading voices from the distance are heard,
Deafening in this precarious night,
The ship cannot return from whence it came,
Down the sinking ship of night,
In furious waters thus went
Forever lost.

The Storm

Daisies dance with the gentle breeze
While the blustery weather increases with ease,
The rain begins slowly, then it pounds,
Upon the ground, you hear the sound.

Clouds, puffy and gray, in haste multiply
Their eerie darkness across the sky,
The winds increase in velocity,
While the rain falls in significant quantity.

Lightening provides temporary light
While thunder entertains this ghostly night
The variety of storm that demands respect,
Mother Nature's reminder of her power to effect.

In time, the winds begin to decrease,
The rain, its power to devastate released,
Mother Nature instructs the sky to give way
To sunshine, telling the storm to return another day.

Winter

I look out the window, there is no one in sight,
Snow covers the valley with a blanket of white,
Keeping it warm, keeping it tight,
Under the glistening snow sleeps the grass this night.

Shrubs are bare with no wearing of leaves,
While the evergreens are still dressed in their green,
Some that have lost their leaves, seeking
Wait until they grow back in spring.

I see a squirrel hop here and there,
Searching for food but cannot find,
Climbs the lonely, white-covered tree,
Then jumps to the branch with food in mind.

The deer with their young trailing behind,
Browse in search of food in the cold of night,
Walk on top of the fluffy snow without care,
Scuttle down the valley to I know not where.

The chimney's coil of gray takes form,
As it works to keep its holder warm,
The smoke of burning wood rises,
In the subzero air it reaches the skies.

I quickly glance toward my fireplace,
Then I see the firewood is almost out,
I shiver with cold as I jump around,
Hopping about like a meadow mouse.

I ready for bed in the silent night
While the whistling wind sings its lullaby
The radiant snow falls to the ground
As old man winter twirls the wind 'round.

Nature's Beauty

Contentedly I sit in my gazebo,
Delightedly reading with zest,
I feel the breeze from the meadow
Come near in this sultry summer day, best.

While the azure sky, pleasant and lovely,
Has not a cloud of gray or fluffy white,
The sun raises the beauty of roses,
Shows its best in this spectacular sight.

I glance toward the lovely crowded pond,
The cool water near the stepping-stone,
While the geese float among their young,
They make their presence known.

Birds endlessly fly the skies,
Flap their wings in perfect formation,
Leaving not a space between them
As they claim their domain in celebration.

I lowered my head in concentration,
Hence losing interest in my read,
Instead thanked the Lord for our treasure,
Of all of Mother Nature's magnificent glory.

Petals

While the rose dances with the gentle breeze,
Perfuming the air with its fragrance sweet,
It drenches my garden with precious scent,
Spreading its petals as it went.

Pure white floribunda rose,
While releasing its petals in merriment,
Travels in air here and there,
Where doth the petals go?

Posies

I came to lend a helping hand,
To make your bed of roses,
Shall not take long to grow,
It will grow into lovely posies.

I will spread some seeds here and there,
You do not have to do a thing,
Then you will see the many colors,
The beauty it will bring.

I will give it love and nurture it,
When it is grown, you will dance with glee,
To see the many roses bloom,
Then you will think of me.

Eyes of Night

While the full moon rises above
The mist-filled wilderness
On this mysterious night,
The wolf packs are heard
In every shadow, howling.
Roaming on the endless horizon,
As they stalk their prey,
Frightening as they may be,
With formidable eyes like the flaming sun,
They dare you to gaze into
Their eyes of night.

Eerie Night

This dark starless night,
Casts shadows in wait on every side,
While candles placed across my room,
Provide darkness an eerie gloom.

The wind is gusting and trees are swaying,
Thunder is roaring, a storm is brewing,
With lightening providing temporary light,
Make it seem day instead of night.

While I attempt to read by candlelight,
In this warm, muggy midsummer night,
I cannot absorb what I have read,
I close my book to sleep instead.

I turn and glance far and near,
I distinguish no one there,
With heavy eyes, I fall asleep,
As I pray the Lord my soul to keep.

The Painting

Viewing a painting on the wall,
I cannot help but be drawn
Toward the right, two little girls,
Facing the window, looking out
With such an air of contentment,
I try to read their thoughts.
Their ghostly images cast
Upon the window's shadow...
The girls' reflections look back in.

The Beauty

Beauty walks like the bird gliding in air,
Shining with the brilliance of a star,
Sunlight beating on her red hair of fire,
Her face a-glimmer blinds mine eyes,
With a smile lovely as a crimson rose,
Eyes luminous as the stars on high,
Profound azure like the sky,
Some that sharp eyes can tell,
She ready this salient day too well.

Summer Heat

While the hot and sticky night,
Offers no relief, no end in sight,
Leaves are still, there is no movement,
No breeze to feel to cure my ailment.

One window opened, fan on overdrive,
Hot air blowing, trying to survive,
The comfort I so acutely desire,
To plunge into sleep but cannot retire.

I lay in bed this clammy night,
I marvel if tomorrow might,
Bring us another sultry day,
With no comfort like today.

While the hours slowly creep forward,
Daylight approaching onward,
My eyes feel heavy as I surrender,
To the heat of the night, I swelter.

This Old House

I am lonely and so empty,
You no longer visit me,
I have been sentenced, condemned,
Stale air of neglect suffocates me.

I feel cold and depleted,
Abandoned and unwanted,
In the deafening silence,
I remain isolated and daunted.

Give your warmth and restore
The beauty that was before,
Give life and love to me,
Before I crumble and cannot be.

The Sparrow

Far above the ground he sees,
A forest in search of a tree,
To place his tired wings to rest,
On the tree of nature's best,

While he is resting on the branch,
In The Haven's Forrest Ranch,
He hears the rustling of the leaves,
Serenely falling near the pansies,

Then he watches the children play,
Cheeringly the sparrow sings away,
He flaps his wings and says good-bye,
Up high, he flies the peaceful sky.

978-0-595-39608-5
0-595-39608-9

Lightning Source UK Ltd.
Milton Keynes UK
UKHW011959200522
403306UK00002B/295

9 780595 396085